Mixing and Separating

Chris Oxlade

Crabtree Publishing Company

www.crabtreebooks.com

Crabtree Publishing Company

www.crabtreebooks.com

Editors: Hayley Leach, Adrianna Morganelli, Michael Hodge
Senior Design Manager: Rosamund Saunders
Designer: Ben Ruocco
Photographer: Philip Wilkins

Photo credits: Mediscan/Alamy p. 25; Bojan Brecelj/Corbis
p. 23; Douglas Peebles/Corbis p. 22; Adam Woolfit/Corbis
p. 17; Dave King/Dorling Kindersley: p. 9, p. 12; Reza
Estakhrian/Getty Images p. 20; Johner/Getty Images cover
and p. 24; Ryan McVay/Getty Images p. 21; Mike Powell/Getty
Images p. 11; Roger Spooner/Getty Images p. 14; Roger
Stowell/Getty Images p. 18; Chris Windsor/Getty Images
p. 15; Jurgen Vogt/Getty Images p. 8; BSIP/photolibrary p. 10;
IPS Photo Index/photolibrary p. 19; Simon Fraser/Science
Photo Library p. 13; Philip Wilkins p. 16, pp. 26-27.

Activity & illustrations: Shakespeare Squared pp. 28-29.

Cover: Two cooks make a cake mixture.

Title page: Mixing two colors together to create a new color.

The publishers would like to thank the models Philippa and
Sophie Campbell for appearing in the photographs.

Because of the nature of the Internet, it is possible that
some website addresses (URLs) included in this book may
have changed, or sites may have changed or closed down
since publication. While the author and publisher regret any
inconvenience this may cause the readers, no responsibility
for any such changes can be accepted by either the author
or the publisher.

Library and Archives Canada Cataloguing in Publication

Oxlade, Chris
    Mixing and separating / Chris Oxlade.

(Working with materials)
Includes index.
ISBN 978-0-7787-3640-0 (bound).--ISBN 978-0-7787-3650-9 (pbk.)

    1. Mixtures--Juvenile literature. 2. Mixtures--Experiments--Juvenile
literature. 3. Separation (Technology)--Juvenile literature. 4. Separation
(Technology)--Experiments--Juvenile literature. 5. Matter--Properties--
Juvenile literature. I. Title. II. Series: Oxlade, Chris. Working with
materials.

QD541.O94 2007   j546   C2007-904322-4

Library of Congress Cataloging-in-Publication Data

Oxlade, Chris.
   Mixing and separating / Chris Oxlade.
       p. cm. -- (Working with materials)
   Includes index.
   ISBN-13: 978-0-7787-3640-0 (rlb)
   ISBN-10: 0-7787-3640-7 (rlb)
   ISBN-13: 978-0-7787-3650-9 (pb)
   ISBN-10: 0-7787-3650-4 (pb)
   1. Mixtures--Juvenile literature. 2. Mixtures--Experiments--Juvenile
literature. 3. Separation (Technology)--Juvenile literature. 4. Separation
(Technology)--Experiments--Juvenile literature. 5. Matter--Properties--
Juvenile literature. I. Title. II. Series.

   QD541.O96 2008
   546--dc22   2007027421

Crabtree Publishing Company

www.crabtreebooks.com   1-800-387-7650

Published in Canada
Crabtree Publishing
616 Welland Ave.
St. Catharines, Ontario
L2M 5V6

Published in the United States
Crabtree Publishing
PMB16A
350 Fifth Ave., Suite 3308
New York, NY 10118

Published by CRABTREE PUBLISHING COMPANY
Copyright © **2008**

Published in the United Kingdom in 2006 by Wayland, an
imprint of Hachette Children's Books
The right of the author to be identified as the author of this
work has been asserted by him.

CONTENTS

Words in **bold** can be found in the glossary on page 30

What is a mixture?

Everything around you is made up of materials. Everyday materials include plastic, metal, water, and wood. A mixture is made up of two or more different materials.

↓ *This is a mixture of nuts and raisins.*

Materials are made up of pieces. The pieces can be large, or they can be tiny **particles** that are too small to see. In a mixture, the pieces of different materials are not attached to each other. We can separate them.

↑ *Pouring this mixture through a **colander** separates the pasta from the water.*

Mixtures around us

Many **natural materials** can be mixtures. Milk is a mixture of water, fat, sugar, and other materials. Seawater is a mixture of water and materials called salts.

↓ *The smoke from a fire is a mixture. It is made up of hot gases and tiny bits of* ***soot***.

← *We can make new colors by mixing two colors of paint together.*

It's a fact!

The air around us is a mixture of gases. One of the gases is called **oxygen**. It is the gas that we breathe to stay alive.

We can make many different mixtures ourselves. We can mix ingredients together to make tasty foods, such as fruit salad, which is a mixture of different fruits and juices.

9

Mixing solutions

When you put sugar into tea, the sugar slowly disappears. The same thing happens when you put salt into a pot of water for cooking vegetables. The sugar and salt are still there. They are mixed with the water.

↓ *The **granules** of this sugar cube will gradually get smaller until they are too small to see.*

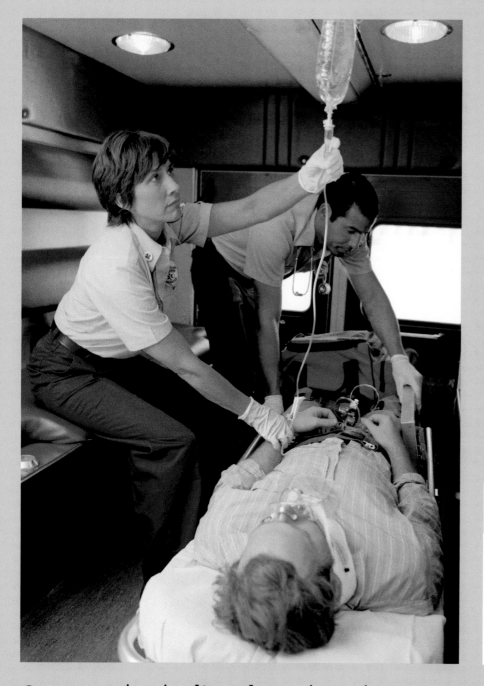

← *Solutions are used in medicine. This patient is being given a salt solution.*

It's a fact!

Fizzy drinks are a mixture of liquid and gas. The gas makes bubbles when you open the can or bottle.

Sugar and salt **dissolve** when they are mixed in water. The small pieces of sugar and salt break into tiny particles. This sort of mixture is called a solution.

Separating materials

Sometimes we want to get certain materials from a mixture. Then we have to separate the mixture.
For example, we separate peas and cooking water to get the peas.

← *This spoon is full of small holes. It is used to separate beans from cooking water.*

↑ *This giant magnet is picking out a metal called "steel".*

We use the **properties** of a material to separate it from a mixture. Properties tell us what a material is like. A property of steel is that it is **magnetic**. We can use a magnet to pull steel paper clips from a mixture of steel and plastic paper clips.

It's a fact!

Tiny bits of gold are often found in the mud at the bottom of rivers. You can separate the gold from the mud by swirling the mud around in a pan.

13

Sieving materials

Some mixtures are made up of pieces of solid materials. We can separate the large pieces from the small ones by sieving. A sieve is like a tray with hundreds of holes in the bottom. When the mixture is poured in, only small pieces fall through.

↓ *The tiny bits of soil fall through this sieve. The potatoes are left.*

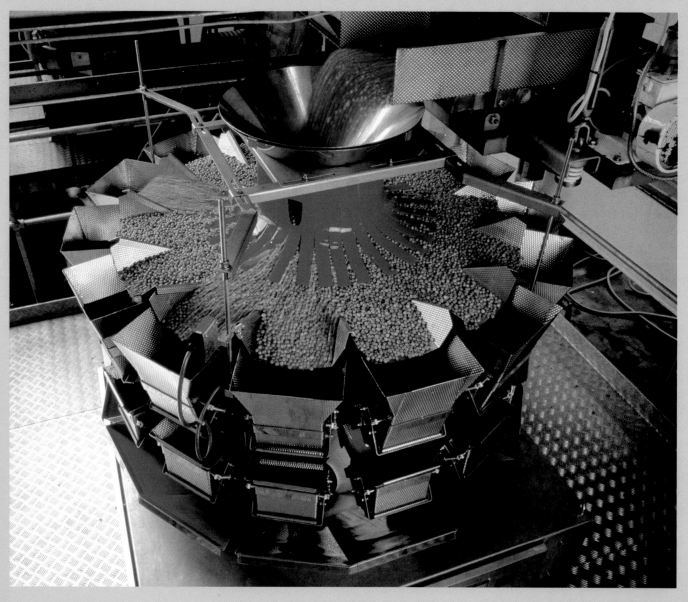

A mixture can be made up of different sized pieces of the same material. We use sieves to separate the mixture of pieces into their different sizes. For example, potatoes from a field can be sorted into large and small sizes using sieves.

↑ *This is a pea-sorting machine. It is sorting the peas into groups of different sizes.*

Settling and skimming

Some mixtures are made up of two liquids mixed together. Others are made up of a liquid and solid pieces mixed together. If we leave mixtures like these standing still, they sometimes separate by themselves. We say that the mixture settles.

← If we leave muddy water standing still, the dirt settles to the bottom.

← *This container of milk will settle to make **curds** and **whey**. The curds will be used to make cheese.*

It's a fact!

All of the dirty water from your toilet, sink, and shower goes to a sewage system. It settles in tanks and the clean water is pumped out.

When we let a mixture settle, some materials rise to the top of the mixture. They make a **scum** on the top. We can scoop the scum off. This is called "skimming".

Filtering liquids

Some mixtures are made up of bits of solid in a liquid. We can separate the solid and the liquid by filtering. A filter has holes that let liquid through but trap the solid. When we drain vegetables through a colander, we are filtering out the water.

← *The holes in this filter are too small for the grains of rice to get through.*

← A paper coffee filter lets water and some of the coffee through but traps the larger coffee particles.

It's a fact!

Campers sometimes have to drink water from streams. They use a water filter to separate dirt and tiny bugs from the water.

Filters are often made of paper or fabric. These materials are made of thin fibers. There are tiny holes between the fibers. When a mixture is poured onto filter paper, the water seeps through, but the solids are trapped.

Filtering gases

Air is a gas that contains dust and other particles. For example, smoke from a fire is a mixture of air and tiny bits of ash. We use air filters to separate the air and the bits of solid. This cleans the air.

↓ *This man's facemask lets air through but stops him from breathing in tiny bits of the harmful material.*

← *The paper filter in this vacuum cleaner traps dusty air. The dust collects in a bag, which can be thrown away.*

It's a fact!

Engines need air to work. They suck air in through a filter. This stops dirt from getting into the engine.

A vacuum cleaner sucks up a mixture of air and dust. Inside the machine, the dust is separated from the air. Filters trap the dust but let the air through. The clean air is blown out again. The dust is stored in the machine.

Evaporation

When the ground dries after rain, the water turns to **water vapor** and mixes with the air. This change is called "evaporation". We can use evaporation to separate the parts of a solution.

↓ *Saltwater is being separated. The water is evaporating, leaving the salt behind.*

↑ At this factory, saltwater is being distilled to make fresh water.

Sometimes we want to keep the liquid from a solution. We do this using a process called "distillation". Liquid evaporates from a solution to make gas. The gas is cooled down and turns back to a liquid.

It's a fact!

In some countries people use water from the sea for drinking and washing. The salt is separated from the seawater by distillation.

Making new materials

Sometimes when we mix materials together, we cannot separate them again. This is because the materials change when they are mixed with each other. For example, we mix flour, water, and other ingredients to make dough for bread.

← To make a cake, you mix flour, eggs, sugar, and butter and bake the mixture in an oven.

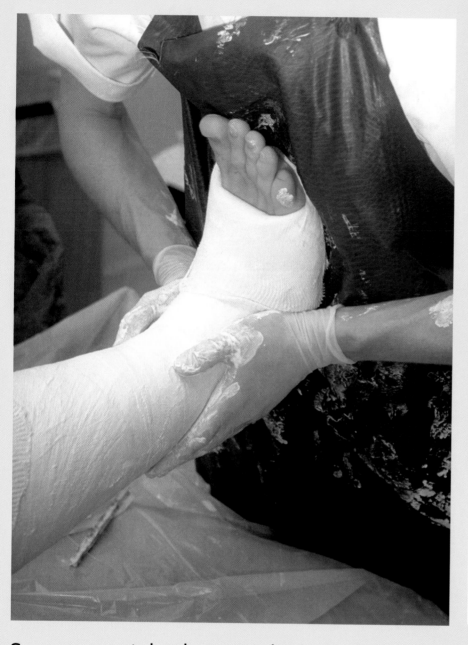

← In hospitals, plaster of Paris is used to make casts for broken limbs.

It's a fact!

Concrete is made by mixing cement, water, sand, and gravel. After the ingredients are mixed, the concrete turns into a solid.

Some materials change when we mix them with water. Plaster of Paris powder turns to thick paste and then turns hard when it is mixed with water. The two materials have changed. We can never get them back.

See for yourself!

Separating with magnets

Try this experiment to see how the properties of a material can help separate a mixture.

What you need
steel paper clips   plastic bowl
uncooked rice   magnet

① Put some paper clips and some uncooked rice into a plastic bowl and mix them together.

② Slowly move the magnet through the mixture. The paper clips stick to the magnet. This separates them from the rice.

③ You can also try this experiment using other materials, such as nails and flour.

②

Settling muddy water

Find out how mud can be separated from water.

What you need	
jar	old spoon
water	soil from the garden

① Fill the jar with water.

② Add a spoonful of soil to the jar and stir. The muddy water is a mixture of water and soil. Always wash your hands after touching soil.

③ Put the jar on a shelf and leave it. Look every hour to see what has happened.

④ The mixture soon begins to settle. Bits of rock sink to the bottom. Rotting bits of plants float to the top. After a few hours, the water becomes clear again.

Super smoothies!

Mixing and making a smoothie

Here is a fun and tasty way to learn about mixtures. You will need an adult to help you. When you have completed the activity, you will have enough smoothie to share. Make sure that no one has any allergies associated with the ingredients listed below.

What you need

1 banana
plain yogurt
blender
orange juice
mixed berries
measuring cup
spoon
drinking cups or glasses

1. Measure 1 cup (236 ml) of yogurt, and scoop it into the blender's glass container. Peel the banana, and break it into chunks. Add the chunks to the yogurt. Right now, you have two solids in your mixture. If you needed to, could you separate them? How?

2. Add 1 cup (236 ml) of mixed berries, such as blueberries and raspberries, or other small pieces of fruit to the mixture. Then add 1 cup (236 ml) of orange juice. You can use milk instead of orange juice if you wish. Now you have added a liquid to your mixture. If you needed to, could you separate all of the ingredients from one another? How?

3. Place the top on the blender's glass container. Have an adult blend the ingredients until they are smooth. Pour the smoothie into individual glasses to share.

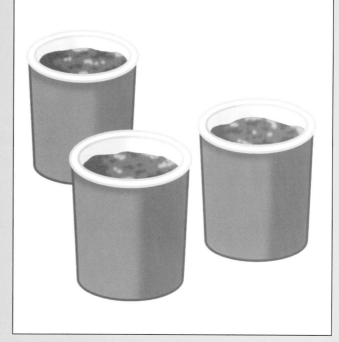

What you will see:
If you blended your smoothie mixture for the appropriate amount of time, it should be a thick liquid. All of the ingredients are mixed together completely. You would not be able to separate your original ingredients from this new mixture. It is now a fruity and delicious drink!

Glossary

colander A bowl-shaped container with small holes in the bottom

concrete A material used in building that becomes very hard when it sets

curds A solid material made when milk is separated

dissolve To break up into tiny pieces in a liquid

granules Small pieces of a material, one or two millimeters across

magnetic A material that is pulled toward a magnet

natural material Any material that comes from the ground, plants, or animals, such as rock or wood

oxygen A gas found in the air. We need oxygen to breathe

particle A very small piece of material, too small for you to see

property Tells us what a material is like

scum A layer of solid material floating on top of a liquid

soot Tiny, black particles of burned material

water vapor Water in the form of a gas

whey A watery material made when milk is separated

Further information

BOOKS

How We Use: Metals/Paper/Rubber/Wood
by Chris Oxlade, Raintree (2005)

A Material World: It's Glass/It's Metal/It's Plastic/It's Wood
by Kay Davies and Wendy Oldfield, Wayland (2006)

Investigating Science: How do we use materials?
by Jacqui Bailey, Franklin Watts (2005)

WEBSITES

www.bbc.co.uk/schools/revisewise/science/materials/09_act.shtml
Animated examples and a quiz about changing materials

www.chem4kids.com/files/matter_intro.html
All about materials, including mixtures and solutions

PLACES TO VISIT

American Museum of Science and Energy, Tennessee
www.amse.org

The Children's Museum of Science and Technology, New York
www.cmost.com

The Discovery Center for Science and Technology, California
www.discoverycntr.org

Index

All of the numbers in **bold** refer to photographs.

Printed in the USA